SHRINE AND ALTAR:

ESTABLISHING

YOUR

PERSONAL SANCTUARY

FOR

SPIRITUAL AWAKENING

SELF IMPROVEMENT AND

DIVINE CONTEMPLATION

HRU YUYA T. ASSAAN-ANU

ANU NATION

BEHIND ENEMY LINES

ISBN-13: 978-0692327913

Shrine and Altar
HRU Yuya T. Assaan-ANU
ANU Publishing
www.ANU-Bookstore.com

HRU Yuya T. Assaan-ANU
"Shrine and Altar"
ISBN-13: 978-0692327913

© 2014, HRU Yuya T. Assaan-ANU
ANU Nation
www.ANUNation.org

LIVICATION

I give honor and strength to all my children, born and unborn.
I commit this work to the heads of my first and last born.
For all of the forces who heed my call and aid the unfurling of
my divine Nia, I also give you this literary libation.

To all the wombyn who come with a heart,mind, and womb to
produce using the seeds of inspired thought that I offer, I honor
you.

Thank You, all.

Contents

SACRED SPACES

I am using the phrase "sacred space" as an over arching term to refer to altars, shrines, temples, and any area that we consecrate and designate for our interaction with celestial forces.

The interweaving of our terrestrial lives with the bodiless spiritual flow that exists in and around us is vital to any creative work. It is this sacred living fabric comprised of the immaterial and the material that shrouds the intense intelligence of the godlike. On the hallowed ground of your sacred space you will learn to weave your own divine cloth utilizing word power, symbolism, alchemy, inspirational movements, and mental imaging. Regardless of the form that your space takes on, you will exercise it as a fulcrum for the push and pull activity required to cultivate your spiritual relationships.

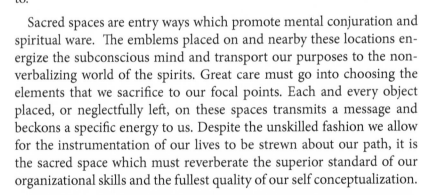

Everyday routine places us in surroundings which, oftentimes designedly, steer us away from our elevated ideas and unbounded truth that we endeavor to live out. Our sacred spaces send the messages of our aspirations on our behalf even at times when we drift far from our centering. It is also the value of the focal points that we create in these spaces that help us to formulate clear images along the pathways of our spiritual psychology. Surviving in the domain where spiritual causation is bartered for physical effect, we can make great use of the tangible symbolic focal points that permit us to peer into the worlds that we desire to travel to.

Sacred spaces are entry ways which promote mental conjuration and spiritual ware. The emblems placed on and nearby these locations energize the subconscious mind and transport our purposes to the non-verbalizing world of the spirits. Great care must go into choosing the elements that we sacrifice to our focal points. Each and every object placed, or neglectfully left, on these spaces transmits a message and beckons a specific energy to us. Despite the unskilled fashion we allow for the instrumentation of our lives to be strewn about our path, it is the sacred space which must reverberate the superior standard of our organizational skills and the fullest quality of our self conceptualization.

There is a strong dependency on the metaphorical value of the gear used throughout our sacred spaces. These objects are the metaphorical, abstract, and literal syntax that we use to command the spirits in our employ and divine with the forces that guard us. The value of prayers and affirmations are rooted not in the lyrical content of said language, but rather in the vibratory and numerical value of the words spoken.

Whatever we choose to do in our sacred space will be assessed by the forces with whom we are communicating with for moving quality and symbolic distinction.

The spiritual kingdom is one of creativity and metaphor. It is through the use of these sacred metaphors that the truth of existence is broadened and reinterpreted in the psyche of the individual. In essence, the symbol that you put at your sacred space today could garner an entirely new meaning a decade from the moment it is placed there. This is because as one's relationship with the celestial bodies intensifies, so does their comprehension of the geometry and deep meaning of the everyday symbols placed before them. So, the metaphors and symbols used at your sacred space are living, evolving representations of your own spiraling journey.

Going forward we will cover several types of sacred spaces, their uses, and methods for constructing them.

H. YUYA   T. ASSAAN-ANU

SHRINE

A shrine is a place that is devoted to a specific energy, purpose, or individual (all of which coming under the precept of a force).

Above all else, you are a shrine unto your higher self.

Shrines can be built and kept up by anyone. Specific initiations or clerical memberships are not requisite. Certain forces may have more than one shrine and those specific shrines may serve particular aspects of those forces. Depending on the dimension of the particular force being enshrined and worked with, ascendant levels of ceremonial initiation may be called for.

A shrine is a place of preservation. In this we are serving as curators for a specific force or entity. Your shrine will often house objects and energies that speak to a single purpose, experience, or person. Consider a shrine a testament. In that you will want to add objects that serve to preserve the idea or vigor surrounding the force that you are enshrining.

Your shrine space is for energies that you desire to cherish and maintain at a certain state.

Anything that we perceive can be preserved, even if only by symbolic design. In fact a shrine is typically a time-based construction. What this means is that with a shrine we are usually preserving a moment or someone/something at a certain moment.

Consider the mortuary arts. Remarkably, the goal of a mortician is to show an individual who has recently transcended their human state in a form that still appears to be human. This is a form of enshrinement.

This form of sacred space, or portal, is an ideal location to commune with a specific energy for the purpose of divination. Historically, an enshrinement would be consecrated to a specific oracle. This spiritual housing would serve to focus the energy and would, literally, house it.

In this design the spiritual aspirant is pulling a force to them. This, alone, is the core purpose of ritual. The shrine facilitates ritualistic activities better than any other space. At this location one is urged to bring what resides in the immaterial world to the world flesh and effect.

Excerpt from ANU Spiritual Training Phase 1 "Shrines and Altars":

A shrine is a dedicated space or experience dedicated to a certain force.

The Shrine:

A shrine is usually designed by the dictations of the energy you are working with. When building a shrine I advise you to tune into the frequency of the force/person you're dedicating it to. I know that when we are working with Ancestors and people we may have felt an affinity for when they walked the physical plain but, it's best to construct your shrines using intuition tuned into the wishes of the forces you're enshrining.

The reason for this is simple. All too often we lock ourselves into a temporal identity of someone based on what stage in their life's development that we've crystallized them at. This is great for nostalgic and sentimental purposes but, on the celestial level our images frozen in time do little to empower the forces we're looking to work with.

Let's consider our Ancestors for this concept. When our loved ones make the transition to the Ancestral realm their physical body stays here on earth. What continues on? They receive a glorified body after their transition and their human identity becomes the shadow. Their spiritual identity becomes the more pronounced character.

Here on earth, for many people, the physical is all that is "seen" and they only see glimpses of the spiritual world. After transition the reverse becomes true. So, your job, as shrine erector, is to attune yourself to the newness of the energy you're looking to provide the gateway for. When people make the transition not only do they transform but, they are always exposed to a new realm of archetypes. Those who transition even receive new spiritual names that coincide with their full spiritual identity.

Performing spirit work is not just about learning the profundity of the ancient but, it also demands that the worker stay on the cusp of spiritual technology.

H. YUYA   T. ASSAAN-ANU

<u>ALTAR</u>

As the name infers, an Altar is used to raise or alter the actual state of consciousness. With that said, an Altar can be constructed and outfitted however your psychology sees fit. In fact, typically an altar will be crafted to fit the intentions of an individual, home, or community in a unique fashion.

Altar styles and construction techniques are oftentimes predicated on the cultural metaphors and symbolic creations akin to a singular cultural group. Even before the cultural group referenced it is the prerogative of the individual to employ any physical object, symbolic representation, or spiritual/corporeal instrument that they deem can alter their own consciousness.

When we strive to raise our vibration or elevate our cognitive state we are speaking of the purpose and endowment of the altar.

Symbolically Altars are often just a series of steps. On each step there may be certain objects and inscriptions that speak to the spiritual achievements and goals for that particular step. It is the emblems that we place on our altars that often can only be comprehended by us alone. It is the prerogative and natural rite of the individual to seek out their tools of spiritual alteration.

The objective of the alter is to leave the human role behind and to hoist one into the space of the spirit, sometimes called the astral realm.

Excerpt from ANU Spiritual Training Phase one "Shrines and Altars":

An Altar is a dedicated space used to alter ones consciousness.

The Alter space is erected to reflect the aspired mental and spiritual state of the shrine constructor. The altar is your personal laboratory for experimentation limited only by the thresholds of your own inner creative vision.

The substance of creation is pulled from chaos. If your alter reflects chaos, do not be dismayed. Concern should be held for Altar, or Shrine, if the space is unkempt and clearly neglected. This is a reflection of the disarray and neglect that you currently have in whatever area of your life that spiritual space is representing.

Typically you should picture your Altar as a set of steps. Your Altar is the space you use to step your spiritual station up. Whatever is needed to raise yourself up to what you see or aspire to be your divine privilege, than those things should be present on your Altar. Of course, this means that your Altar may not look like any other you've seen before; as your own personal challenges and desires should uniquely reflect those in concordance with your life purpose.

ANCESTRAL SPACE

An ancestral space is usually the first attempt of the newcomer at establishing a spiritual focal point in their home.

Applying our innerstanding of shrines and altars we can now see contrastive uses and designs for our sacred ancestral spaces. Commonly we would use a shrine to celebrate or house ancestral energy but, an altar can be used or a combination of both.

When we are working with our ancestors at our sacred spaces, in fact, we are working with their spirits. The ancestral soul, willfully, goes back to its place of origin. The realm of the ancestor is housed and sustained by the spiritual intention sent forth from those still in the third dimensional scape of the living. Ultimately all spirits are thought projections. It is our projected idea of the ancestral memory that allows that supposed specter to take form in the realm of the deceased.

Sacrifice is the staple nutrient for those in the ancestral realm. What we send to that kingdom furnishes and augments the veracity of it. With that thought any force can be made sacred and sent to the ancestral kingdom. In various traditions around the world, when someone of great power and rule transitioned to the ancestral world their tomb would be furnished with all the objects that they would need in the kingdom that they would soon arrive at (this would sometimes even include their living servants). In this example we see the objects that would be buried or encased were actually sacrificed. Despite the exploits of tomb raiders, the general consensus was that these objects were not to be used for earthly gain ever again but, rather sacrificed so that they could be used for gain and navigation through the tract of the afterlife.

SHRINE ALTAR

H. YUYA   T. ASSAAN-ANU

THE BASIC ELEMENTS

Establishing a sacred space can be a daunting task. The best way to initiate the process is to keep things as simple as thinkable.

Surely, many of us have seen altars and shrines that are adorned with elaborate artifacts and symbols. Your first shrine should have very humble beginnings. One of the basic templates you can use in building your shrine is to model it using the six elements.

Depending on the nature of your sacred space, the element will take on a different significance.

FIRE

Fire and Air are masculine principles. In similar fashion they do not trans-mutate with the matter that they come in contact with, unlike water and earth which integrates into the alchemical process (feminine absorption). Fire is not born of the matter that it effects but, can be an artificial contrition and deliberately stirred up.

Fire affixes itself to the body and aura of a spirit. We perfect our fire via the genius of our meditation. Meditation work at your sacred space has a direct effect on the depth of your transmutation. Consider a set of ingredients. It is through the use of fire that we typically are able to see the purifying effects of true alchemy and observe a substance going through various states of being.

Fire can liquefy, solidify, and even turn matter into vapor.

It is the entire essence of who and what we are that is purified and our state altered through our fire. Fire doesn't seek to separate us from our internal parts but, rather congeals all of the parts together. So, in that, the whole of what we are becomes a pure representation of our souls and spiritual station. Those things that are foul and the aspects that we hold virtuous all become a part of the purity of our being. It is our wholeness/perfecting that is achieved through the element of fire.

Your Pineal Organ, or brow chakra if you will, is also referred to as "The Lamp of God". This is the highest star of your body and the ignition of this fire is what guides our perfecting work. It is the force of imagination that ignites this sun star. Exploring the mythology of the Gin/Genie and Solomon/Sun-Of-Man, we recognize that it is Solomon who holds authority over the Gin by use of sacred symbol and incantation. Our personal Solomon is none other than our brow chakra. It is the power of our ima-GIN-ation that transports us to the dominion of Solomon.

Fire will corrupt, purify, generate and perfect all at once. It is an element that stands alone but, at the same time can be generated by contrition. If added to material substance it has the potential to be expanded and augmented but, its basic nature will still not be corrupted via interaction with crude matter, unlike other elements.

When working with fire and seeking color equivalents red, white, and black serve best. These colors represent the various states that fire will carry matter through. This also means that metals that associate themselves with these colors can be used as representations of our desire to spiritually conduct fire.

In our Kabbalistic systems we see fire at the commencement of all things in the form of "Ain Soph Ur". The meaning of the phrase is "limit-less Light". Light is derived only from a fire of some sort.

Fire is your precious and essential individuality. It is the unchangeable force within us all. The esoteric form of the kundalini serpent.

Representations of Fire:

Candles, incense, breath, physical activity, friction, electricity, the color red, the color white, the color black

Uses on the Shrine:

Fire can be used as an indicant; informing us as to if the energy that we are working with is actually present.

For those more sensitive to visual stimuli as opposed to other types, fire's excitability to spiritual current can serve an essential purpose. When working at a shrine we are usually pulling a singular energy to us or exchanging energy with a singular energy. We can use the flames of our burning apparatus to determine if there is spiritual activity in our space. A flickering flame shows spiritual activity. Fire that has difficulty staying lit or that leaves an abundance of soot in its shute or holder, shows a force that it is coming up against in which it does not have power directly to surmount

Light, as offered by fire, also serves as a navigation anchor for spirits seeking to find their way to you. The light is no different from a guiding star, or light house even, guiding travelers to their destination.

Uses on the Altar:

On the Altar, fire is commonly sustained by using a candle or incense, however cadenced breathing can raise the fire within the body temple to adjusted states of consciousness. When we pinpoint the direction of the Northeast we see a combination of fire and air. This warm air serves as a tool for ascent as warm air is used to elevate objects. Heat placed on that plotting, next to an emblem of the air element elevates the spirit. Fire breaths can also be used to this aim, while focused on this direction.

Gazing into a portion of flame, changes the brain wave patterns of the participant. Gazing into a flame has long since been a tool used for hypnosis. The patterns of delta, theta, and alpha have all been measured via EEG apparatus during candle gazing activities, while performing non-directive meditation. This lack of direction sends the gazer into the overhead fire of imagination.

Water

As fire is an active energy that seeks to launch out and be seen; water is a passive energy that calls us to look into the aspects of being that may seem murky and unclear. Water represents, not only, change of life but, it is also a carrier for the conscious vibrations that ripple at singular points of disruption.

As fire expands and engages, water contracts and shrinks. Similar to the energy of Earth, water is the energy of vibration and depth. In the fixed forms utilized in physics, water represents motion. It is the emotional pool that water expresses. Emotion is energy/electricity in motion.

Moving bodies of water offer us the symbols of innocence and the renewing of youth. As it is said, "You can not step in the same river twice". Water reminds us of the constant motion present in the universe. It beckons us to acknowledge the value of flow and current. Current can be connected with the material idea of currency of wealth.

Water is a substance that is pregnant with life and possibilities. Water in various locations lends a respective message. For instance, water of the sea (Olokun/Poseidon/Neptune) reminds us of the fertility of those locations and the constitutional fertility of the subconscious mind, or underworld. Water as found in a waterfall reminds us of its purifying and illuminating potential. Water of a murky swamp would speak to stillness and mystery.

In our Orisa tradition, there is an archetype known as "Yemoja". This title is a combination of Yeye- Omo-Eja. Yeye meaning "Mother", Omo meaning "child", and Eja meaning "Fish".

Let's look at the symbolism of the fish for a moment. The fish symbolizes the passivity of the water element. Many species of fish are only defended by a slippery body, and quick movement. Defensively, the fish has a vibrational connection to all other sea life by way of the womb-like water body. The fish never swims into conflict but, always looks to move from it or around it. It shares a connection with danger via the very substance in which it dwells. There are no hiding places and movement is done in groups, in a seemingly unpredictable manner.

Water lends itself to chaos and unpredictability. Water is an amalgamate of individuals and nations. As nations are built upon waterways, it was the great Fela Anikulapo Kuti who reminded us of the duality and unpredictability of water. He told us that no matter what we do in life we must return to the water, even if it has caused us great loss or harm. It is the value of returning that water also represents.

Even in this returning, water still declares its independence and fluidity as its cradles and sea floors go un-manicured or molested by the designs of those from above. Free will is typified by the flow and psychic vibration of water. Water offers no boundaries and no hindrances from one point to another.

In ancient KMT there existed and archetype by the name of Tefnut. Tefnut was partnered with the archetype Shu, a force of the air. It is through Tefnut that we see the itemization and the commemoration of the traveling state of water known as "moisture". Moisture has the potential to travel through and get into any environment, even without intentional entry way. The driest of environments still posses moisture. It is in this idea of moisture that we see the principle of fertility and revival. We are connected to all things animate and inanimate, by the value of moisture.

Consider the concept of "Emi". Emi is defined as divine breath. This is the breath that was called upon in the Helios Biblios/Holy Bible at location Ezekiel 37:1-14. This commission that the God of Ezekiel places on him to speak to the valley of the dry bones was a call to impart divine breath into a population of hardened and deaden individuals. It was a call for revival. It is the re-hydrating nature of water that can be used to bring objects back into the land of the living. There is no creature or person who comes into the world of the living who does not pass or gestate within an environment of water, first.

Water absorbs and connects us with the world of feelings, soul, fertility, fluidity, and psychic ability.

Representations of the element of water:

Any fluid, the color blue, the color white, water heavy fruits and vegetables, herbs and plants that grow in or near water

Uses on a Shrine:

Water is a receptacle and container for spiritual energy so therefore water on a shrine can be used to house the energy it is that you are working with. This can be as simple as pouring water into a cup, bowl, or even on the shrine itself. If you are enshrining an energy that is a patron of the water element, the use would be obvious. Just the mere placement of water on the shrine would inform that energy that you have set a place for it.

You can also use water as a looking mirror. The water surface serves as a gateway between worlds. This gateway can be offered as a portal for an energy to come through or return home through, after affirmations to that affect are said over the body of water.

Uses on an Altar:

On an Altar water can be used to transmit an idea, for divination, and even to send herbal messages to yourself. For example, if one were suffering from disease, they could place water on their altar and infuse it with various herbs for healing or conscious altering. They could then peer into this medicinal libation and mark the images which come to mind. They can also use this water as an entry way into their own psyche or as a representation of the entry or exit of womb energy.

Water is also used to elevate the position of a person, place, or thing. You can use water on your altar as a defensive tool by placing a representation of yourself into the water and then raising the water level, by adding more water to the receptacle. By doing this you are sending a message to the higher parts of your own psyche, or the energy being aimed for that you desire to be elevated in life and supported by the maternal fluid of water.

Air

The principle of air represents a distinct dichotomy of polarities exclusive to this moving element. Air has the potential to carry fire in the form of warm air and it can also be a conductor of water in the form of moisture.

Air is the typification of frivolity, intelligence, and positivism. Air strives towards the properties of optimism and innovation. Out of all of the known elements, with the exception of ether, air is typically the most misunderstood. Interestingly enough, though all of the elements are the progeny of Ether, air is closest in nature to it. If Ether is the energy of the soul's source, and water is the reflection of the soul, air is clearly the spirit nature.

We use the element of air to support and propel our causes into the majesty of our high notions and ideas. Air offers us intelligence because the bulk of this element is exposed to light. In fact, air is the element that is allowed to flow closest to the intensity of the sun.

Air quality improves as we increase elevation. It is in the places where we find high rock faces, hillsides, and natural elevation that we find a superior quality of air. The physical characteristic of this quality of air reflects the lucidity of thought and inspiration that is found when thought vibrations are elevated. There is a sharp clearness of cerebral activity and function. When the mind is clear, the pathways to the greater spiritual knowing are cleared.

In our Yoruba culture we have an archetype known as "Esu". This archetype governs many things but, one of which is the quickness and brilliance of wit. Esu is the holder of "Ase". Ase being the manifestation of the divine breath into the form of spiritual authority, life force, and power accessible to those sojourning the red road known as "life". This power is the reinforcing element for all that we perceive in existence, material and immaterial. In applying this reference the reader is urged to grasp the truth that air is the element that dominates the elements of water, earth, fire, and metal. Air reigns with greater power through its ability to influence the other elements.

Air at a state of stillness is life giving to the persona; being. In movement, we refer to air as wind. Wind has the ability to augment the vigor of fire. Wind has the ability to dry water or advance it in the form of moisture. Wind also has the ability to erode the stoic power of earth. Wind can even mangle and erode the unbending force of metal. Wind can not be contained.

White, silver, or gray are the colors that provide the insignias for the air element.

Air typifies the state of being that many of us aim towards. It is the abandonment of the human brain activity and conscious mind that allows for the clarification of the high idea and spiritual vision. The transition from air to wind mirrors this notion. This holds the same symbolic value regardless if artificially produced, or if it comes as a product of nature's discretion.

Wind is the activation of thought. Dissimilar from imagination which associates itself with the idea of fire, wind is the movement from brain to mind, from reflexive function to alchemical thought. The value of this element is unseen but, always felt. Air is in constant contact with the auric fields of all in existence. Similar to the water element which permits consistent contact with all people of the sea, it is the element of air that removes all barriers that may be attempted between those who live and function on the transforming plane of earth.

 Those who thrive in the element of air are, more often than not, seen as arrogant, lost, irrelevant, and even "crazy". It is their ability to pull away from the manicured social programming that affects the earthiness of the body and human brain activity that puts them in a unique place of the unseen element. In this we realize that air/wind is more spiritual than it is corporal. It takes us all into a place where we can view our unseen, and intangible, ideas and talents in order to express them through the other elements.

Wind is not a passive element. It is a property of great push. Though its life giving state of air lends itself to the lungs of all people, it is the aggressive propulsion of wind that manipulates all other elements.

Air carries the aroma of all other objects to the noses of earth's people. In this we see the value that it can serve to manipulate the reality and state of being of the individual. An herb, resin, bark, or oil does little by and of itself. It is not until its aroma is carried to us on the wings of wind that we are able to experience its remedial or offensive properties.

__Representations of the Air element:__ Incense, fans, feathers, the color blue, the color white, windmills, breath

Uses on a Shrine:

Wind is a conduit for messages from the ancestral realm. Because there are few places air will not travel it can be used to send messages to a large group of people/forces or to an energy that is seemingly out of reach. The breath of life falls into the domain of air and can be used to enliven an entity so that you can communicate with it via your shrine space. This is done, automatically, each and every time you recite an incantation, prayer, or affirmation. The combination of air and moisture animate energies in need of that form of power (Ofo Ase).

Offerings that are to be sent to a particular energy can be sent via wind currents. In this we can utilize the aromatic and, even, smoky quality of herbs, oils, resins, and the like. Even medicinal herbs can be placed on our shrines and the smell or fume of their burning parts can be sent towards our objects of spiritual communion.

Uses on an Altar:

On an Altar the element of air is valuable in our movement towards a more lucid and free thought space. The earth itself is an altar. It is a means of ascension. Left to its own, air will rise and stir. The simplicity of watching the rising smoke of your incense supports this sacred visualization.

Also, the inhalation of various aromas and herbs can propel one to higher states of consciousness. It is the act of smelling that which is carried through the air or filling the air in our lungs with certain stimulants that can raise our overall vibration.

Focused breathing also helps to remove the focus and concentration on the physical abode and escort the psyche into a more still place of clarity and anticipation.

Earth

Earth is the cold, dry element. It is the receptacle for all of the gifts that we affirm for from the realm of the north, or spirit. The earth is the place of grounding and pragmatic toil. Stability is the nature of the earth element and the conviction and resoluteness of one's objectives.

We use the esoteric, and even physical, element of earth to ground and anchor us. Grounding is crucial in any, and all, spiritual work because there is an intent to abandon when going into the spiritual psychology. Thought is abandoned, concerns are abandoned, ego, the body, etc.. The earth element reminds us that we are apart of the natural pantheon of the planet. It calls us to be true to our nature and to cultivate it as a farmer cultivates a field for production.

The earth element is also a catalyst for the thought of manifestation. It is the place where we actually go beyond the position of being and into the process of doing. The earth element demonstrates our creativity, physicality, endurance, and commitment to the things that we say we are. This feminine element brings solace and peace through its science of moving meditation. In that the act of "doing" becomes the entry fee into the mysteries of the earth element.

As the earth element being a feminine element holds the mysteries and depth of all feminine principle, it is this planetary gender assignment that reminds the practitioner of their own depth. The earth element represents the hidden power, resilience, resources, and endurance that all humans have the capacity for.

Despite the awareness of these vast pools of talent, wisdom, and power the earth element glides us to the floor of practicality and reason. Earth is the cool dry space that snuffs out or cradles the fire of impulsiveness. The earth element is not "boring" by any stretch of the imagination. In fact it is this element where the unseeable reserves of strength are applied to the imagination of the fire element to create a glorious blaze illuminating the self actualizing practitioner.

The earth element reminds us that we are here to bear fruit. The reflection of the divine force is shrouded in an earthen body of water and earth but, its image is seen by all via the earth element. It is what we produce that discloses the quality of our own wisdom. If wisdom is water and the produce is earth; the earth requires good clean water in order to bring forth good clean produce (understanding). This water is purified by the element of fire. The quality of this entire process is made evident by the manifestations that occur in the earth realm. This is the realm of the real where we face the true fruits of our labor or the rotten stench of our own inequities.

Holding the earth element dear is necessary in order to move from the stasis of analysis and rebirth through the canals of application. We experience the corruption of life via the earth element and through this we strive for a more perfecting experience. On the planet diligence and consistency are required in order to fully reap the benefits and the potential energy given to us from the north, where the seeds of heaven may fall. Organization and gather herald the arriving of an earth season or spirit; as does the series of cause and effect.

All energy of Alchemy come in contact with the earth element and the majority are either fruits of the earth or housed by it. The very idea of an element typically leads us to the greater appreciation of the steadfast properties of the earth element. It is here that we begin our process of the transmutation of the proverbial, and literal lead. Lead being the soft, malleable, but weight metal that serves as a base for the journey to the conducive, glorified gold element. Although these elements exist in the vast family of metal, they owe their maternal reverence to the element of the earth.

Earth represents culture. The earth is the housing for all ideas produced by the human and spiritual mind. It is on this planet that the cultivation of the person takes place through the transformation of their minds. This transformation is a result of contact with heavy, dense, obstacles along their path. The earth is a neutralizer of energies. It is through this neutralizing that individuals are afforded the opportunity to go to zero point once more and advance their journey towards self realization, courtesy of the element of the real.

beginning / lowest form of energy.

Representations of Earth: Soil, rocks, crystal, resin, wood, metal, the color brown, the color green, plant life

Uses on a Shrine:

Plants on a shrine surround furnish us with another instrument of divination. The state of health that your plants exhibit will render evidence of the state of spiritual health that the focal shrine energy is experiencing. One need not even use a plant to utilize this energy. A pot or bowl of soil can also be used to receive libations, offerings, and concrete the vibrations of the affirmations said into the soil, as well as the fluid that is poured into the soil. *actually planting your crops like seeds. WoW!!*

Crystals on a shrine can also be utilized to house an incorporeal entity. All that we realize are crystals of some form with varied vibrational frequency. Crystals hold memory. They house the intelligence of the planet, the individual, and the spirit. Spirits are thought forms and thought forms are spirits, therefore within each and every crystal one may acquire, there exists a spirit, and that spirit retains a wealth of cognition. On an altar, crystal can be used as domicile for spirits, a conjuring point, meeting locations, and even a key to the varied realms that the spirits you desire to connect with reside in.

Uses on an Altar:

Earth is a component of attachment and anchoring, serving the purposes of conscious ascension as a protection tool on your alter. When the spirit travels, the encasement of the body is left and the distance between spirit and the body is increased. In order to remain connected to the organic structure; metals, crystal, and even stones are commonly attached to the body of the astral traveler or placed on the altar of the astral traveler.

Stones are often used to build the shrine itself. Stones or crystals are synonymous with the rock face found on hillsides and mountains. The mountain associates itself with the idea of climbing, opportunity, and elevation. In animal form, this is symbolized by high altitude animals such as the goat, eagle, and ram. Any part or representation of these sacred animals can be placed on or near your altar in order to attract the energy of earth, ascendency, and opportunity.

Ether

Ether is an all powerful substance of de-constructing and simulation. Whatever ether touches, it completely subjugates and takes it through a procedure of transubstantiation.

Ether serves as a receptacle for all of the gases in our environment, those natural and those unnatural. It is the cause of all things and forces. Ether descends upon life, while concurrently receiving the karmic product of life and the wisdom gathered from it.

Ether is the cause that serves as the quintessential sub-context of all other energies. Ether has been considered to be the fifth element. The prefix "Quint" as used in the word "Quintessence" or "Quintessential" derives its designation from this notion. The author would like to take this time to place the idea at the feet of the reader that ether is the first element. It is the cause for all causes and the essence of all things perceived and unperceived. As the Brow Chakra is no more a "third eye" but, a "first eye", Ether can be no more a final element but, the primordial one. Ether is feminine in nature, destructive and life giving, typifying the poles of this substance.

The element of Ether produces all elements and contains the properties and characteristics of them all.

It is in the term "Ethiopia" that we see a cause of Ether. The term "Eth" means to burn, sully, or singe. This is the fiery aspect of Ether. In the name of Ethiopia we speak of a "burnt or singed" people, similar to our term KMT (Land of the burnt faces).

In our Kabbalistic system we have the sefirot known as "Keter", often pronounced and spelled as "Kether". Notice the formation of the word "Ether" within its spelling. The K, as in the term "Knight" signifying the mystery of hidden aspect of the letters forming the word following it. The writings of the Zohar inform us that "Keter" serves as the source of all things and is called the "Dark Spark" or the "Dark Flame". It is the light that is incomprehensible and beyond human apprehension but, serves as the abundant source of intention and sustenance. Even in Biblical lore the term "Ether' is defined as "abundance". Kether associates itself with one of the names of the creator known as "Ehveh", meaning "I shall be". Ether/Kether is the boundless potential that our imagination and force of will pulls from in order to create the reality we choose for ourselves.

Ether is the staple substance of all creation and the untouched, form-less consciousness which reigns supreme over all elements, similar to the crown or "Kether/Keter" in our system of Kabbalah. The crown rep-resents the authority of an individual that said individual has no ability to comprehend. The crown rest itself on the head of the person. This indicates the influence and spiritual ordination/positions that we are given in life that are invisible to the perceptual experience of our hu-man-like thought. It is above thought or above the ORI ODE (Yoruba – Outer head).

Chemically, Ether is an organic compound which has very little reac-tive quality. Ether is a stable compound but, at the same time a com-pound of infinite variability. It maintains the composition formula of Oxygen, Carbon, and Hydrogen (the last two forming as hydrocarbon), the same substances used to create carbohydrates, commonly known as sugars. It is the "sugar" in the form of ribose that serves as the backbone of Ribonucleic acid. It is this substance that serves as one of the core building blocks of the reproductive genetic element.

The centering molecule in the classes known as "Ethers" is the oxygen molecule. In alchemy the element of Ether is often depicted as a circle, although there seems to be no set or official symbol for the element of ether. The oxygen/"O" is the passivity of this compound while the akyly groups, usually depicted by the letter "R" are the functioning composites of the Ether class. So, even in the chemistry of the element we see the quality of forcefulness or motionlessness.

Our spiritual value for Ether lies in its abundance principle of realiza-tion. This is the element that we employ for the creation matter of what it is we mentally envision as our soul aspirations and the supporting substance for the reconstruction of our reality. Ether is akin to the clay on the potters wheel of Khnum.

Ether is the point of burning that exists inside a vacuum of water trav-eling a non-breathable current of breath.

Representations of Ether: Womb fluid, menstrual blood, sperm, the element of ether, carbon, coal

Uses on a Shrine:

Ether is the force that we tap into in order to join with the forces that we seek to commune with. It is the energy of ether that facilitates the assimilation and evolution of one energy to another. Ether absorbs all that it touches into its formless void. Once this ingestion and digestion occurs, it is Ether that augments the nature of the entering part and brings out its latent power.

This kernel of creation can be utilized to create a spirit entity out of the womb of one's mind or the physical joining of an actual womb and staff. All things come from the ether so, despite our exertions to construct a reality based on what we perceive, it is the dark unknowable constitute of Ether that orchestrates the chaos of creation beyond the scheme of the conscious mind.

Uses on an Altar:

Ether is the highest aspiration and the deepest descent. Elements of ether abound but, the substance is not utilized without the querying of the soul. Ether is not a component that can be assessed from the outside in but, must be conceptualized via spiritual and mental alignment with the advance of the soul.

Ether holds a place of honor on the altar of any entity because, it is Ether that they all birth from. Unlike the other elements that can create spirit, and embodied material; it is Ether that has the ability to circumscribe portions of the greater soul force. This occurs through the use of sexual intercourse between man and wombmyn, with focus being on the crown chakra. This is also made possible by the life giving divine breath and incantation, all of which increase the activity of chi, life force, or Ase. These substance heat up when active.

The manipulation of the hardly controllable Ether comes with greater spiritual experience and proficient. As Ether seeks to assimilate all that it touches, it also can easily control the mind of the neophyte spiritualist.

Metal

The use of metals on your sacred space ties the practitioner with planetary energies, bodily functions, and spiritual properties. They serve as an excellent conduit for the various shades of a force. Metal is the containing principle that houses and even flavors the waters of our being. Few things can come into contact with metal without out taking properties from it.

Metals are often overlooked in spiritual work as they are seen to be implements only used in alchemy. In truth, the entire process of establishing a sacred space and sacrificing certain objects to be used on said space is a process of alchemy. The practitioner need not look far in order to grasp the notions of how metals affect the human and spiritual being. The excess or deficiency of certain metals in the human body can lend a person to a state of disease or wellness.

Many metals go through a process known as radioactive decay. In this we know that metals are not "dead" objects but in fact go through a corrosive process while here on the planet, just like the human, plant, and animal kingdoms. Metals can be influenced by their interactions with other elements in the environment. At times this process is referred to as natural radioactive decay, corrosion, rusting, or even oxidation. When this occurs those metals can even change into other metals with new properties. Some metals will rust or corrode and in doing so will take on many of the properties of salt. This now connects that base metal to the esoteric properties of the soul in that there is a presence of sulfur or salt; each of which being key elements in the practice of alchemy. Many metals are greatly affected when they interact with sea water. Some are more vulnerable than others. Even in the process of decay, or corrosion, the corrosion of the metal itself can serve as a thin layer of protection for the principle metal itself. Metals will also tug at one another when placed in proximity with one another. It is the sharing and pulling electrons that causes the metals to change.

When utilizing metals in conjunction with our sacred spaces we can create new life (corrosion) utilizing the different techniques to change the metals. Also, the properties of said metals will speak to our own planetary associations and character dispositions.

Metals are impacted by other metals, earth, wind, and water. It interacts with its surroundings as any other constituent.

Note: The use of metals have similar use whether used on shrine or altar.

For the shrine section I will list several metals of the alchemical foundations and share their properties. I will let the reader use their inventiveness from that point forward.

Representations of Metal: Construction of any fashion, ore, tools, electronics, metal working

Uses on a Shrine:

Gold is the energy of the sun representing spiritual alchemy. Gold, reds, and yellow are the colors associated with the metal gold.

Silver is the energy of the moon, representing intuition and emotion/ white, cream, greens

Mercury is the energy of the planet Mercury representing quickness of wit. The colors associated with this element are silver and yellow.

Copper is the metal of the planet Venus and rules over the conduction of the energy of receptivity and magnetism. The colors associated with copper are blue, pink, and copper.

Iron is the energy of the planet Mars and stimulates the masculine energy of warfare, fertility, strength, and new beginnings. Red, silver, and brown are the colors associated with the metal iron.

Tin is the metal of the planet Jupiter representing the first breath of the newborn. The induction and awareness of the soul. The color white, black, and orange represent this metal.

Lead is the energy of the planet Saturn, associating itself with the heavy dense feeling of rigid duty and the weight of deep thought. The colors associated with lead are black and any color of dark hue.

Uses on an Altar: Metal symbolizes advancement, technology, and cultivation, and the demanding process that we put ore through in order to fashion tools, vehicles, and the implements of technological progress.

Any form of technology represented on your sacred altar sends the message of advancement. Technology should be a support for our spiritual work, not an interpreter of our fundamental sacred communications and spiritual sways. We call forward the energy of technology to remind us that invention and innovation is the heavy call of the spiritual worker.

H. YUYA T. ASSAAN-ANU

Acknowledging the evolving times that we all live in is the charge of a responsible spiritualist. While we surround our altars with the implements of natural primal energy, it is also important to include symbols of progress and evidence of the innovations that can come from the employment of the natural divine forces which surround us all.

SHRINE ALTAR

CONSTRUCTION OF THE SACRED GATEWAY

Where to put your sacred space

Positioning your sacred portal can be a difficult task if your space is limited or there are divergent spiritual views within the same household (see "Solutions for Dysfunctional Family Relationships").

Fortunately, there is no set way for you to preserve an energy, work with your ancestors, or alter your conscious vibration. Ultimately you must do what will actually work for you. This must take precedence over information gathered externally, even if that information is from supposed "experts", this author included.

Let's look at some ideal shrine and/or altar constructions.

Altitude-

For your shrine it's advantageous to place it at a height that requires you to stoop in order to service and make contact with it. This, of course, has a psychological value in that it reminds us to show reverence for those people/moments that we consider precious enough to cherish in an enshrinement. Also, the changing posture causes a break in our commonly held body positioning. This, within itself, can be a great help for those not in a spiritual environment for the majority of their day. The stooping, kneeling or sitting shifts the body and reminds us that now is a time to shift the mind.

Size-

Your sacred space can be as large or as small as you desire. It can be removable, and does not even need to be in or near your home.

Placement of sacred objects

When considering where to place the various objects on your sacred space, it is never a bad idea to work with the Geo-orientation known to you. Determine North, South, East, and West.

In our Ifa/Orisa systems we acknowledge that light comes from the east, water the west, air, the north, and earth in the south. The center position is reserved for the practitioner (Ile Ife – "The house of love"). If one were to look at their own physical orientation, it can also serve as a guide reference for the orientation of objects in, on, and around their sacred space.

Starting in the <u>South</u>, what we'll observe is that what lies directly beneath us is the earth element. What is southern, or below, will eventually lead us to earth as long as we are on the planet.

In the <u>North</u>, as we go above we travel to the world of that which is lucid and invisible. It is the realm of free-movement; even the vehicles that traverse the open skies are not subject to speed limits. This is the symbolic region of spirit free-dome (free thinking).

The <u>East</u> is where we face the rising sun. It is the new day and the force that all soul carriers on the planet strive towards, even through sheer biology. We grow upwards and, for some, the very hair on their heads strives upward; towards the sustainer of life on earth. Our eastern region houses the bulk mass of our heart. The east is the left side of the body. Consider the left hemisphere of the brain. This side of the brain provides us with our pathways and personal tools of logic, linear thought, reason, hierarchy, contrast, literature, and lyricism.

The <u>West</u>, or right side, is where we face the death and transformation of our relationships. In this world we must relate, on some level, to all around us in order to conjure a perceptual experience. When we consider the right hemisphere of the brain, we can see this hemisphere that looks for the law of similarity, and not contrast. This sphere of the brain mass governs our ability of intuition, abstract notions, the concept of "show and prove" (demonstration over proclamation), and fluidity.

First imagine yourself as a living, walking, breathing representation of the sacred space. The sacred space should mirror you. If you do not find yourself in your religion, spiritual practices, and divine ornaments you are in the wrong space and not your true orientation.

As a base template, if you are facing your sacred space you can place the water element to the left, the fire element to the right, the earth element closest to your vertical position centered horizontally, and your air element furthest from your vertical position centered horizontally. The center position should be a representation of the ether element. It is the unknowable aspect of yourself.

It is valuable to place the metal element in the front of the sacred space, build the space out of metal, or have it represented at the four corners. It is the metal element that will serve to protect and cultivate your sacred essence.

The purpose of your sacred space is to align and balance your spiritual faculties by communion, ritual, and sacrifice. In this your spaces, should reflect the spiritual body that you possess. It is this dimension of your being that makes your work conceivable.

If you are unable to place the objects on your sacred space using the orientation model afforded you by your known direction, then go with intuition and start simple. You have a head, you are the master of your own vehicle of spirit travel.

H. YUYA T. ASSAAN-ANU

MAINTENANCE OF THE

SACRED SPACE

Excerpt from ANU Spiritual Training Phase 1
Lecture – Shrines and Altars:

Whether we're talking about the shrine or Altar there are certain "rules" that I advise you to apply.

Always tend to your Shrine/Altar. This doesn't mean that you have to lay at your spaces for hours everyday waiting for a message from heaven but, there should be some level of interaction. A really simple way to maintain contact is to mix a spray mixture of water and whatever herbs or alcohol are in tune with the energy on your shrine. Here are some of the libations you can spray or pour on those spaces:

Hot Energy (Pupa): Ogun, Oya, Sango, Esu, Aganju

You can use Florida Water, Cayenne Pepper, Rum, Gin

Cool Energy (Fun Fun): Osun, Yemoja, Obatala, Osoosi

You can use plain water, rose water, lavender water, efun

Ancestral Energy: Egun, Babaynla's, Iyanla's

You can use Rum, Florida Water, Beer

You can use plain water for any of the energies at your sacred space, whether hot, cold, or ancestral.

Another simple way to keep energy flowing to and from your sacred spaces is through the use of music and incense. You can play music at a certain time throughout your home and offer the vibrations to the energies residing at your scared spaces. Incense and candles are also a simple way to offer energy to these spaces, as well. Your Altars/Shrines are like Automatic Teller Machines; from there you can leave deposits and make withdrawals. The more deposits you make the more force you to pull from later so, make consistent deposits. It's just that simple. You needn't always perform elaborate ritual to feed the forces that work with you. The more you make consistent deposits the more you'll find yourself surrounded by good fortune and swift manifestation of your wishes.

It's just as simple as blowing your cigar smoke onto your Altar/Shrine space or spraying a herbal mixture across that space, daily.

Mold and fermentation on your Shrine/Altar is actually not a bad thing, as many people think. Mold or Chemical process is life. It's actually the burgeoning of new life in this you are creating spiritual energies infused with the aim of whatever that offering/space represents. Objects should change and morph that are on your Shrine/Altar. These are the most powerful offerings you can have on that space. For this reason it's advisable, when possible, to establish your sacred spaces outdoors. If you're able to do that leave whatever you place as an offering, infidelity. The ASE builds over time by itself. Indoors, this is much more difficult unless you're a fan of rodents...

On another note you can always employ the services of cats to help you to maintain your personal spaces but, of course you have to teach them not to feast on your Altar/Shrine offerings.

Your inspirational Shrine/Altar space should not be used as a conversational piece but, should be given the respect and dignity afforded to any living being. Allow your space to be as simple or complex as it need be, designing for crowd appreciation is foolish. Let this space represent the opportunity that you're giving to yourself to be 100% authentic and vulnerable to your own reality. For this reason, many choose to construct their Shrine/Altars in places that offer the least exposure from "outsiders".

Excerpt from Grasping the Root of Divine Power:

ESTABLISHING YOUR

GATEWAY

Jingili – Gulimancema term from West Afraka translated in English as "Altar"

Aforemuka - (pronounced: Ah four-ray Moo-kah) is a Twi word translated in English as "Altar"

Tambiko – Ki-Bantu term translated in English as "libation".

From here on we will utilize these Afrakan terms.

A Jingili is your personal spiritual focal point. In this segment I'll provide some foundational techniques for establishing your portal but, do not be afraid to intuit what your guiding spirits would like to use in order to establish the two way communication that you aspire to have with them. Once you develop some proficiency with the divination techniques outlined in this book, you'll be able to even query the entities that you're honoring through your Jingili as to what they'd like to experience at your sacred space.

An Aforemuka can be placed on a table or on the floor. I would suggest you start on the floor and once divination proficiency is achieved you can question your Ancestors as to if they'd like to be elsewhere.

These are items I recommended to collect for your Jingili:

• **Water** – Water serves as a spiritual receptacle and can be used to scry into; for water meditations. Water serves as a representation of one of the 4 major earth elements.

• **Candle(s)** - The Candle flame serves as a "lighthouse" for the spirits that we are beckoning to commune with us. Spirits are attracted to flame. Also, candles are wonderful for scrying into to focus your intentions through fire meditations. Candles can be used for prayer rituals. They also allow us to represent one of the 4 major earth elements (fire).

• **Plants** – This signifies the resting place of the Ara (body) of our Ancestors and is a representation of life as well as one of the 4 major earth elements (earth).

• **Pictures** – Paternal/Maternal Egun/Amadlozi /Nananom Nsamanfo male and female should be portrayed. Photographs and images assist in focusing our attention and are a way of honoring those who lived and died in order to make space on the planet for our arrival.

Caution: Do not place any pictures of living relatives on your Jingili. This could quicken them to the Ancestral realm.

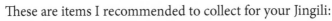

• **Incense** – This is used to clear the space of malevolent energy and to stimulate spiritual communication/mind-set. I'd recommend Frankincense, Myrrh, Sandalwood and even burning powered herbs that were favorites of the Egun who are on the Altar (Cinnamon, Curry, Basil, Rue, KWK....).

• **White Cloth or wooden Mat** – A wooden mat serves well for Aforemukas placed on floors

*All items should be cleansed with sea saltwater and smudged

I'm also partial to a Jingili that incorporates articles that were used by your Ancestors (perfumes, bracelets, charms, smoking pipes).

Crystals are also a great addition for your Aforemuka.

*You can write a list of desires and goals and place them on your Jingili but, I'd suggest you turn them text side down in the event that your Aforemuka is exposed to public observation/scrutiny. If your desires and goals are your own you should hold them close to your heart in a sacred/secret way.

** A friend of mine needed to establish an Aforemuka in her home but, was concerned about her family members who resided with her who saw this method of spiritual expression as "spooky" and sinister. I created a movable/concealable Jingili for her out of a kitchen cabinet. I laid the cabinet length-wise on its side and installed two small luggage padlocks on the side of the cabinets. She was able to install all of her spiritual paraphernalia inside of the cabinet and using the open cabinet door as additional space. This allowed her to perform all of the needed Jingili work and meditation and when finished close it, fasten the locks, and cover it with a piece of fabric. This was a perfectly acceptable/appreciated solution.

Once we've gathered our materials it's essential that we cleanse the space that we'll be using to establish our sacred portal. Take a moment to note that this Jingili is not to double as anything other than what it's been created for. That means do not allow your guest to leave their drinks, keys, umbrella's, plates of beans and rice, bottles of Henrock or EZ Jezus, Four Loko, bootleg DVD's, mail, or anything else on it.

Cleansing your space -

Spiritual cleanses are an important part of divination. It clears the vision and makes us more attractive to benevolent spirits.

1st – cleanse yourself.

Take a bath or shower, first, to remove the physical dirt from your body; I recommend using Black soap for this purpose. Once that's completed, proceed with the spiritual cleanse.

You can perform a simple spiritual cleanse using:

White Rose Petals

Florida Water or Rose Water

Sea Salt

Spring Water

*Also see the section "So Fresh and So Clean Clean" for more baths

Mix the ingredients of the bath in a large natural container.

Light a white candle.

Take the contents and pour them over your entire body from the crown of your head downward.

While doing this, visualize the spiritual sludge loosening its grip on your body and falling to your wayside and down the shower drain.

Some baths you do not rinse off. This one you will as its purpose is to remove harmful energy.

*You can take this same bath mixture and sprinkle it on the floor of the room that will house your Aforemuka.

Once you've removed any harmful energy from yourself it's now time to consecrate the space for your Jingili. Walk throughout your space and get a feel for where your Egun may want to be; perhaps facing a window to the East where they can view their home, or on a sunny back porch where there is plenty of fresh air and plant life, maybe the family room where they can be at the center of family activity.

I would strongly advise against placing the Aforemuka anywhere sexual intercourse may occur. Sex in front of an Aforemuka will "heat" things up in a way that could be exploited by watchful spirit energies and misinterpreted as an intentional ritualistic procedure; in fact sex is a ritual...every time. It's not that sex is an impure act but, it is a powerful act that can direct the energy of a space or unified intention with great Ase behind it. If you perform this act in front of an Aforemuka without proper preparation and incantation you're putting your head into the proverbial lion's mouth.

If you have to set your Jingili up in your bedroom, use a white sheet or wardrobe divider to separate the spaces. A closet can even be used as long as that closet is dedicated, solely to that purpose.

In order to clean the space I'd suggest you first do a thorough cleanse with a pine cleaner (see "So Fresh and so Clean Clean" for this). Clean the floors, walls, furniture, and underneath your home furnishings, as well. While doing this open a window in order to provide an escape route for energies that are being expelled from the home.

Smudging

Smudging is a process of "smoking" the space out with an incense or smoky substance. Malevolent spirits do not like smoke and will make their exodus in the presence of it. To smudge, sage is a great plant that can be used and can be found in natural food markets, "Botanicas", and can even be grown.

You can even go outdoors and use dried tree leaves or dried herbs to smudge with. As always, let your ORI direct you.

*Frankincense is quite effective for this purpose.

As the smudge substance burns pray/speak/meditate over it asking your Egun/Amadlozi /Nananom Nsamanfo to remove any malevolent energy from your home and usher in energy that is healthy for your welfare and development.

After we smudge, we are now ready to assemble our Jingili.

*If possible I would suggest cleaning and smudging your entire home before establishing your space. This is not an instant process and may require a few days of work and preparation but, it is well worth it.

During the construction of the Aforemuka wear clothing that represents the strongest vibration of Ancestral veneration possible. I would suggest Afrakan peace-drobe/attire. You can even wrap a white piece of fabric about you or for men; a white piece of fabric can be tied at the waist.

*OUR Egun/ enjoy aligning with us, more, when we dress in the pat terns and motifs that honor them.

Now, it's time to bring together the pieces of our Jingili.

Everything should be cleansed in a sea saltwater solution and smoked/ smudged thoroughly. You can also wipe them down with an essential oil.

Again a Jingili can reside on a table or on the floor. I, personally, suggest the floor as the Egun like to be close to the ground. In some traditions Egun shrines are even placed in bathrooms or in places in the home where there are pipes that lead into the ground.

Let your own ORI/Egun guide you to what is most correct for you/ them.

Most will tell you to use a clean white cloth for your shrine. This is a good starter point for your shrine as white gives the Egun/Amadlozi / Nananom Nsamanfo a "cool" space to convene. It also represents purity and new beginnings. Many of OUR Egungun have died horrendous deaths and were not given proper entombment rites so, whenever possible we want to invite them into the most sacred and purest environments that we can produce.

Feel your way through the placement of objects on your Aforemuka as you will instinctively arrange the items in a way that allows you to maximize its power as a spiritual/cerebral focal point.

I would also suggest not placing anything synthetic on your Jingili, if it can be avoided. I typically use only organic substances. So, my pictures are framed in metal or wood, water is kept in glasses or calabash, food is served on earthenware or wooden bowls, KWK...

Once your objects are arranged on your Aforemuka it's time to call your Egun/Amadlozi /Nananom Nsamanfo to the sacred space.

1. 1st Light your candle on your Aforemuka.

* The amount of Candles you place on your Jingili can vary as some will place one candle for every Egun represented or others will place 7 candles and 7 glasses of water for the 7 major religions. I suggest, for now, you start with one white candle and one glass of water. Make sure all stickers are removed from the candle if it is in a glass shute and it's been washed with salt water.

2. "Tambiko" is a Ki-Bantu word translated into English as "Libation". This step is crucial in the process of reconnecting with OUR Afrakan source and grasping the root of OUR collective divine power. We should

use OUR Afrakan names for OUR high order deities and Egun/Amadlozi /Nananom Nsamanfo. In doing this we are able to pull from the eternal spiritual pool of the original beings of this world and the next. There is no need to de-emphasize the importance of calling OUR revered spirits by their proper name. Remember the title of this series is "How to be an Afrakan". For a de-cultured oppressed people this concept can be bloodcurdling. The culturally retarded have been trained that it's best that we warehouse the culture of OUR ethnic origins in closets, shadows, musty basements and strive to be as inclusive as we possibly can. When pouring Tambiko, innerstand you are inviting your Nananom Nsamanfo/Egungun/Amadlozi to you.

Do not be ashamed of your lineage. Align with your Nananom Nsamanfo/Egungun/Amadlozi, and they'll align with you. No people show shame of their origins like dispossessed Africans. No Rabbi, Iman, Pastor, or any other professor of religion compromises for you; there is no need to do it for them or their followers. It is treasonous to your culture and Ancestors.

Pour your spring water into your receptacles that you've placed on your Jingili.

Take that same water; dip your middle and ring finger of your right hand into it and sprinkle the water about your sacred space and Jingili reciting Adura 1 and Adura 2 from the "Initiating the dialogue" section of this book.

You are now ready to meditate at your Aforemuka or recite words that invoke the blessings and protection of your Egun.

I would suggest your service and maintain your Jingili daily.

The water that you put in your receptacles can be allowed to evaporate. I see this as the Egun getting their full drink.

You can also use this space to appropriate meals to your Egun/Amadlozi/Nananom Nsamanfo and present your Adimu (Offerings).

If you put flowers on your Aforemuka, make sure they are changed out when they wither.

*Tip – I like to take the shrunken dried flower petals of my Jingili flower arrangements and use them later for smudging. Remember everything that sits in this consecrated space is charged with Ase. Recycle when/where you can! This honors the divine.

Optional Aforemuka paraphernalia:

Skulls – Represent the temporal nature of the life journey and our connection to our Egun/Amadlozi/Nananom Nsamanfo.

Rum – Loosens the tongue and eases the mental grip that sometimes can prevent spiritual fluidity. Rum is also a drink of celebration.

Jewelry – It's good to leave your body adornments on your Jingili in order to charge them with the Ase of that consecrated space prior to wearing them.

Books – Books retain and project the power of their words. By putting them on your Aforemuka you amplify the potency of the messages they convey. Use books that hold special transforming meaning to you.

Flowers – Spirits love flowers.

Fruit - This represents the fruitful harvest that the spirits have always provided for you and will continue to provide.

Dolls – These are focal points that are infused with the energy of your Egun/Amadlozi/Nananom Nsamanfo. They should be treated as living beings....because they are.

Aumba – The Aumba is also known as the Opa Egun or Igi Egun. This is a wooden staff/branch which is used to call the Egun forth as well as to banish harmful energy.

The Aumba is used to assist in summoning your Egun by tapping it on the floor before your Jingili.

*I would suggest consulting with an Elder to have an Igi Egun properly consecrated and fed for your use. Depending on the circumstances different types of Opa Egun are required.

SHRINE ALTAR

H. YUYA T. ASSAAN-ANU

CONCLUSION

The effectiveness of the work you do is directly linked to the degree of confidence and creativity you bring to the sacred space. The moment you put your hand to designing, constructing, and maintaining your shrine or altar, you are creating a world with the balance and mental images that you see fit to. At the moment you feel unsure about what to add to your sacred space, listen to the small voice inside you. Your space may call for objects you have little knowledge of or you've not see on the sacred spaces of others. Keep in mind, the energies that work with you come from a larger pool of spiritual forces but, their purpose and appearance in your life is an incomparable one.

As the custodian, defender, guardian, and protector of this newly created world, its practicality and, even cleanliness, will reflect the reverence you hold for your own spirituality. Once again, YOU ARE THE SACRED SPACE. You are one of the sustaining forces for the spiritual children and Elders who come to your sacred space to commune with you. Do not take this responsibility lightly. Certainly a shrine can be a show piece of elaborate adornment. In this you are giving even more honor to the energy that you are working with. An altar is a very personal portal and you have every right to keep it hidden. Your life need not be an open book and the depths of your power does not need to be public record.

Do not be afraid to blend similar representations of energies from what you perceive to be different spiritual systems. There is a hierarchy of spiritual forces and as they descend on the planet the realization of what they are is re-translated by the populaces who come in contact with them. The shape of their power is documented to the degree directly proportional to the degree of boldness the individual holds to look outside one geographic location or religion. Allowing the reception of a larger family of spiritual intelligence allows us to receive a more robust picture of what the individual spirits and forces are. There are no monopolies on universal energies.

In this work, I deliberately avoided making polarizing statements as to the rules and regulations of shrine or altar construction. If one is mature enough to become steward of a sacred space, then they must also be mature enough to own, boldly, the ideas and inventiveness that they attach to the sacred space.

It is my supposition that it is time for the shrine/altar model to take on a new expression and role that reflects where we are, as a people, today.

I do not teach religion but, rather serve spiritual templates to the greater body of portioned souls.

Endeavors to embrace the archaic methods of our ancestors of yester-year are admirable, however all things must evolve using the knowledge, wisdom, and over-standing of our ancient predecessors and guardians. We have no concrete proof informing us that we have not seen the golden era of our spirituality. Your generation may truly be the one to master the process of turning the dense lead mentality of the collective to the electrically charged gold mind-set of the deities so many beckon for at their sacred spaces.

Your DNA ladder is the altar of your soul, your head is its shrine.

It is time that we all manifest on a level worthy of the moving quality of our own spiritual thought and mental alchemy. I will that this work has moved you, at least, one more step into that direction.

Your Brother,

Yuya

ABOUT THE AUTHOR

H. Yuya T. Assaan-ANU is an initiated Priest in the Nigerian Orisha tradition and an advanced student of the IFA priestly order, as well. Yuya has been working with the spirit world through various indigenous native systems for over 20 years as a spiritual counselor and guide. He is also the Chief Priest and temple head of "ANU Nation"; where he has initiated a cadre of students into Orisha tradition as well as his own ANU Spiritual Order and currently teaches indigenous occult and mystery systems, African philosophy and spiritual sciences, and divination to adults as well as children through his school, "The Sadulu House Spiritual Center."

Books:

Chief Yuya is also the author of "Grasping the Root of Divine Power", "Solutions for Dysfunctional Family Relationships", and several other forthcoming titles.

Classes:

Yuya teaches classes on spiritual growth, personal development, and indigenous ancient spirituality. Classes are taught in three phases and bring a person through the beginner to advanced level of spirit and soul work in a very hands on practical manner.

To enroll in a class you can go to SaduluHouse.com.

Connect with Me Online:

Twitter: http://twitter.com/hruassaananu

Facebook: Facebook.com/h.yuya.assaan.anu

ANU Publishing: ANU-Bookstore.com

ANU Nation: ANUNation.org

Radio Broadcast: EnlightenmentandTransformation.com

51210296R00043

Made in the USA
Middletown, DE
30 June 2019